Presents

Written by Jamila Gavin

Illustrated by Rhian Nest James

Grandma was on the garden bench.
She looked up at the blue sky.
It was like the blue sky in Pakistan.

Grandpa was in the house.
He looked out of the window.
He saw a red car.
'Uncle Sami and Raza are here,'
he said.

Ali and Amina went to see
Uncle Sami.
They ran to the car.

Uncle Sami got out of the car.
A girl got out of the car too.
'This is Raza,' said Uncle Sami.
'She is your cousin.'

‘Come in, come in!’ said Grandpa,
and they went into the house.
Uncle Sami had a big bag.
Raza had a big bag too.

‘Here are some sweets and cakes,’
said Uncle Sami.
‘And I have some presents for you,’
said Raza.

Ali and Amina jumped up and down.
'What have you got for me?' said Ali.
'What have you got for me?'
said Amina.
Raza put her hand into the bag.

‘Here is a shirt for Ali.
Here is a Shalwar Kameez for Amina
and here is a waistcoat for Grandpa,’
said Raza.

‘I have a present for Grandma but I can’t see her,’ said Raza.

‘Grandma is on the garden bench,’ said Grandpa.

‘Grandma,’ called Ali.

‘Grandma,’ called Amina.

‘Uncle Sami and Raza are here.

They have a present for you.’

Raza went up to Grandma.
'This is for you,' said Raza.
Grandma was very happy.
It was a blue shawl,
blue like the sky in Pakistan.